FORCED CONTINUITY

MIRIAM E.WALSH

BOOK 3: RANDOM SERIES

ardornata
publishing

Cover art by Miriam E. Walsh
Book design by Miriam E. Walsh

ISBN 978-0-9836598-2-2

ardornata publishing
www.ardornatadesign.com

Table of Contents

About The Author

Miriam E. Walsh has worn many hats to pay the bills:
mental health worker at a detox unit, drafter in the engineering field
and graphic designer --- but she has always donned the hat of a
poet.

For many years, at her home on the south shore in Massachusetts,
she has tended to many writing projects, the culmination of which
is the Random Series of books.These poems have been written in
many places; lunch breaks, poetry readings, train rides and, yes,
car rides!

She has been published in U.M.Ph.! Prose Online and is a regular
fixture at local poetry venues including "Poetry: The Art Of Words
Mike Amado Memorial Series" in Plymouth, Massachusetts.

Miriam E. Walsh has an BS Degree in Psychology from
Bridgewater State College, where she also minored in art. She is
an accomplished photographer/visual artist and a member of the
Plymouth Arts Guild.

random series
book 1 : beautifully alien refraction
book 2 : primitive awe
book 3 : forced continuity
book 4 : small lucidities

my mouth 04

it is the hot
inside my nostril
and the tightening
of my lower jaw
in contention,
crushing any words
that had the foolishness
to hesitate there.
neurons ,tongues and air
are their limited
habitats;
as air born viruses,
skin absorbed oils
that sink seditiously
through hair follicles
and sweat
or sexually transmitted
addictions

they cannot survive
in the rapidly changing
climate
of my mouth
with its
gnashingsmilinggrowling
tasting
all the ways
that I drown there.

disjoined 04

i pull back my eyelid
with my finger
and glimpse
the inside
of this pink pocket
I am floating around within,

the configuration
so relied upon
for my sense of reality,

loosely bound sack
of water and calcium
floaters
tangled in twisted tributaries
of veins and arteries.

all threatening
imminent failure
with their bruising;
the way the warmth
retreats from my fingers
in winter
and the panic
of my tear ducts
cannot distinguish
a physical pain
from this emotion.

atoll, a toll 04

i remember
being desperate to love.

hollow
without another
filling me
a wanting
needing definition
in its satiation

a meteor collision,
a crater
a scarred earth.

forcing up
dark depths
drowning
tropical forests
in ash,

unfeeling fury
of a perfectly natural
occurrence:

disaster.

a continental shriek
an atmosphere suffocating
with debris

but its trauma
eventually faded
with dew drenched flowers,
entangling canopies
of chlorophyll created night
sheltering the slithering,
the crawling,
the grasping

something has grown there.

indivisible 04

i am
glimpsing distantly;
this grief
is relief
that somehow
i can still acknowledge
absence.

a knowledge
that has not left
me
though all i thought
was wisdom,
has.

halved itself
and then again,
and then again,
until it is the last
infinitesimal
point
indivisible.

coil 04

and glistening
is the glowing
of what we think
are holy eyes.
holes
an unblinking
focus
upon the inevitable.
swallowed, swallowing
blind
in consuming everything.

a line of lip,
a ceaseless seam
of oceans horizon
fading into night.

my mortality
a coiling creature
around my larynx
tightening

and yet my breath
carries
through a constriction
that my voice cannot.

ent-eyes 04

and there it was again
that precise glint
upon his eyes
so well placed,
so it seemed
that they were illuminated
from within.

was it meant
to make her feel
this much a child,
this helpless,
this drunken.

she could barely

keep her knees straight,
without becoming
an awkward
tripping collection
of extra limbs,
a cataclysm
to the delicate balance
of the trapeze act
arrangement of
papers on the desk

did he mean to
be seducing

with that gaze?

no
it was just a communication
a simple
payattentionIwantyoutoknowthis

but in the polite
request
encoded
in the widening
of a pupil
and the drawing
of a smile....

you're making me
enjoy you,
and i'm not sure
i want to enjoy that...

massachusetts driver 04

raindrops
egg broken
sizzling on my windshield
yolk open
a new thought
wiped away
i make it through each morning
by pushing everything aside;
the rain,
the cars,
the worried dream
of an hour ago.

i plow through them
at 20miles over the speed limit,
piercing the wind
to rupture the gray
of this morning.

,
gas tank's full
fear is my fuel
turning me into a froth
of sharp teeth
bearing upon the other drivers
as the hypocritical politik
lies to me from the radio.

I know better than this.
but I won't behave better.

I know the signs
30,50,60
and I know
that none of them matters
when no one is watching.

I will do what I want
in a world
that will do
what it wants with me.

the only thing I am sure of
is my tires, my grasp
but these things
have been known to fail
on slick roads, on slick
words

I know only one word
in sign language

and it is for everybody.

avoidance 04

this heat has all
the texture
of uncaring
my skin is drenched
and weighted
on every breath
pulling the sky
so close overhead
that I can't stand up
straight.

maybe I'm just tired.
maybe.
maybe this insomnia
is the buzz of insects
outside
grinding me down.

the change in my pocket
makes me part of the 8%
who have a chance,
yet the green of my eyes
is growing greener
with the red surrounding

telling me even so,

that I will not make it.

I want for nothing
I want nothing

but want is the only
thing to pull my steps
from me

I'll stop for
morning coffee
so I can start
and so
I can pretend
that the engine
isn't seizing

that all I have done
was all that I could've done,
all I should've done,

but I've traded
an avoided slavery
for this one.

worship 04

your eyes levitated
upward
into the most
beautiful accusation,

a widening pupil
swallowing my fear
a lake
quietly receiving a stone
enveloping it
in descent.

I could not see
the sea
floor from my reflection
and the listening, glistening
of your stare,
and the rare ripple
from each thrown word.

but you could see
me
a lidless fish
worshipping the
turbulent sparkling
of the sun,
from behind the pull
of the tide
and membrane of blue

a star
wanting to douse itself
in sunset.

unshattering 04

enlightenment
was such
a average state for you,

smiling with
a lazy yawn
in a sun saturated boredom
of it
knowing better to play
as spiraling leaves
and
crackling twigs
in distant scampering.

laid bare
in low-lid unblinking
a floating
seeking solace
in the grass,

focused upon
a point in the sky
the border of
a wisp of cloud,

and then just beyond.

finding humility
in the 3/4 illumination
of moon,
the sphere it implied,
the dangling in black.

feeling the earth shift
like a disturbed christmas
ornament
that someone
had just shuffled passed

and this day
was just one more
merciful unshattering.

daemon 04

1. also demon, an evil or malicious spirit (religious)
2. supernatural being acting as an intermediate
*   between gods and human beings(greek myth.)*
3.a process / program that operates
*   in the background (unix operating system)*

this is not real.

i hear moth wings
fluttering
from a river in west virginia.

its eyes behind
the static, the (s)now
of an end to a broadcast day.
the blue of dawn
hovers outside my window
with its expectation of sun
and eventuality of night.

if I look at it long enough
I think
I will catch it flicker.

the shadow
of the window washer,
a wrinkle in the program
being adjusted
from the other side
of this equation ,

manifested as a ripple
to a fish knowing only
ocean

mammalian 04

the sky cracked
and i was awake,
a pulsating mist
of light
and ever transmuting fury,
a verbal humility
for widened black eyes
in their burrows.

one more day
in this bubble
of blue
now reminding
its inhabitants
of what rupture
sounds like,

when the blackness
outside
is pounding on the
back of sky

the friction of molecules
jarring, colliding
for a place in this jar
this safety;
a rare solace of earth.

it threatened the roof
of this house;
all the intricacies
i rely upon.

the light,
the ground,
a constricted breath;
my mammalian sense
of continuity.

09.20.05

even in
black and white
from the far view
of centuries end,

all these
beautiful faces,

still
shivering
in a wind
carrying its cold
to my skin , now,
but my eyes are warm
with the pink
and the pulses

of such
beautiful faces,

still
lips
speaking upon yours
the silence
that all of us hear

simon,

sleep well
among
beautiful faces.

in color 06

your eyes
saturated pink
to the flickering
of black and white
and how just now
you realized
that just because
it didn't happen
in color,

doesn't mean
it didn't happen.

that our films
grow grainy and worn,
the past
is an atrocity
for mannequins
not the warm
pungent pulse
next to us
on the subway,
in the rain,
or lounging
on a sunlit common.

those things
just don't happen
in color

detritus 05

"you *are* good..."
shuttering, wincing
to the thought of such
self-luminescence,

a breath in bracing
as if in falling
staring into
some midpoint
just beyond
your eyes
floating following
your heartbeat
to the ground
as a recently
traumatized tremor
now settling,

such an admission
forcing other
possibilities, futilities
upon you
stealing away
the ease and comfort
of being broken,

and all else
unfractured.

imaginary 05

i am missing you
before i meet you.

saying goodbye
before i destroy
that which i have
never touched,

before it touches
me.

and you never
actually existed,

just my version
of an imaginary friend
to people my hours
and the distances
that i feel expanding
my every cell,

separating me
at a most basic level,

even as the
tail of your tune
repeats in my
periphery
structuring my thoughts
in a tangling
around its blindly
relentless dance.

in plain sight 05

start from the eyes
natural coverage
and hypoallergenic
over the pink,
over the black,

running;

blending back
to match the tone
of much more
practical parts
(of you)
the ones that
never cry.

my first lesson
was at eleven
when i was told
not to make a scene.
that somehow
my tears could do
much more than
wet my face
(when they obviously
meant so little)

so from then on
i secretly
used my mothers arsenal,
the tools all
women are trained in

the art of disappearing
in plain sight.

curio[us] 05

you grab
my hand
to pull my eyes toward you,

to see the atoms
travel up my arm
into my dilating iris
displacing each other
in arching, outward ripples
until the pattern
of defenses
is spread
and splaying,

a floating flower
of a frozen firework
faceted and reflecting
every fold
and fissure,

illuminated with
the refusal
in your eyes
to leave me
where i live:
in a more constant
and comfortable
configuration of me.

rather i be
curious
than a curio.

the painted 05

the silence with its fingers
again
making the air
full and compressed
within my throat

but somehow
allowing
me to breathe
again.

all this loneliness
is making me in love
because my eyes
have stopped assuming
and now i am
seeing the peel back tabs
on the edges
of every thing;

the model houses,
the actually empty graves,

the painted.

and i am smiling
at all i thought was real
because now
all that i believed
can't possibly be true.

that my nightmares
have no more flesh
is enough
since i would have
consumed all that i love
anyway.

again
i find myself
a pin point of light
cradling myself
with this lullaby
and dozing
to the creatured dances
dangling above me;
the flickered shadows
in the next room
of this chalice mind
convinced the they
are the murmurs and motions
of a caring god

so my lids can fall
and the dream
can start
again.

forgetting 05

in this rain
the wind is swirling
in my cochlea,
an ocean
in a conch shell;
and this night
has given me clarity
to hear only
the sounds
of small things.

the drops crackling
on the pavement,
a dog's bark
echoing
at the scent
i am giving off for miles,
and the glimmer of a bulb
on soaked leaves
burns my eyes
with the crispness
as if i was
staring into a cluster of stars
being born in a nebula.

such things
my weathered mind
sees
more directly
than my sheltered one
does from its windows.

and my skin
shivers,
my muscles remembering
themselves
in this
forgetting.

mating ritual 05

your hands
are loving
a soft pressure
on my shoulders
making echoes
and carrying signals,
each follicle alert
and then
shaking you off

for my shiver knows
that you do
not love me.

it knows
in all the ways
it registers cold

as it does now
sensing the outer shape
of your breath upon my neck.

each pore
a module of elaborate defense
closing, contracting
with all the reflexes
that all fingers
have taught me,
shooting out bristles
to keep you
at an escapable distance
as my eyes
exude and ooze
a venom
in a long indifferent stare

of your own reflection.

and i leave you
a mewing mate
kicking up sand
for me to answer back.

unaccompanied 05

an ever-present
thought:
i am alone in this world.

but this ache
is not searching
for an anesthetic
in pleasantly distracting
company
or the appealing symmetry
i am suppose to be
wired for as a floating
pheromone programs
and initiates my next move.

i am not just lonely
but unaccompanied.

this morning
the equation
was written and
translated
through the static
of my radio
because it was the
only thing
not lying to me

my birth-my death
and the in-between
means nothing

no
i am used to
non-god's silence
and stars living out
their billions
winking out of fusion and habit
and not at me.

yes
i am used to
being small before the sky

it is that i am
even smaller
before you.

tomorrow 06

she kissed
as if blessing,
as if tasting
to recall
at a later date
of anticipated
hunger

to slowly
release
what was behind
those lips
in a perfumed exhale
of her own.

so the air
could carry
its survival

its scent
drowsed her
into a tomorrow
that wasn't
there before.

starfish 05

a starfish
reaching for
distant suns
with the innate
knowing that
i have been given
the right shape
with the wrong skin.
the heavy membrane
of the material,
a bumpy creviced;
injured and injurable,
housed in a hardened
place.
and waiting
to dissolve.

reality 2.0 05

i am a fat man's
floor shrieking
barely supporting
the tension,
intention,
is a thing i can't afford.

choice is the latest download
reality 2.0

is that why i cant be happy
because i dont have
the latest games and tricks?

does my video wall
have the right scripts?

only the sun reminds me
that the ultraviolet
is not light and that
i am an outdated tool
obsolete to the elite.

this awakening
is making me cruel
in all the things
i want to die,
i want to destroy,
with my own hands

and i feel the pressure of
it upon my palms
just to be sure
i am a broken bird
shivering in my
own cold fingers
i have not managed
to conserve even that
much kindness.

i want to feel me crushed,
i want to feel my hollow,
avian bones collapsing.

can i relearn mercy?
is it like young skin

never had again?

is it as simple
as wind, warm or green
or is it
an atlantean myth
as exaggerated and
as exasperating
as the boney models
in women's magazines?

my throat closes upon
the idea
i am nothing
or
i am very important

but i cannot
figure out how,

i feel as pock marked
as the moon
from impacts
that i am still
shaking from.

big boys 05

gridlocked and corralled
by other cows,

i am a creature raging
for release.

beneath my calm
my everyday,
drugged with a dart
and my sleeping limbs
i feel the blood
punch through
the numbness,
a solution a needles
and shattered glass
puncturing
every cryogenic
ganglia
just dangling there.

i am using fear
this morning
instead of it using me.

god's sons
make a standby threat
of what can be done
to my vagina.

an ultraviolet
that is suppose to
kill my cell's center
so the DNA can be rewritten.

i'll just use it
to get a tan
and make
my skin into leather

less pleasant
for you to fuck.

all the while
you're screaming
that you are not
your father

because your haircut
is different
and you don't have
the same tailor.

such rebellious sons,

seeking shelter
in the same brand
of cruelty
with a different
manufacturer,

just to prove
who's got the bigger bomb
and
who's the bigger antichrist.

such big boys.

geocide 05

mother must (die)
because you will not
have us
have any other gods
but you.

and here
comes a tiny predator
that always wants more
starved of its
original meaning
by those
who named Magdalene
a whore
so every child
will have no womb.

a knife kept
mid-piercing the heart
pulled just short
of bleeding
to a perfect depth
of control.

a just may happen.

i'm sitting here
with a playing
internal script
what i imagine
to be an average.
insanity

what makes a person's
thoughts
crazy?

a committee?
an unfashionable god?

or is it all just
a murder
with billions
of accomplices
naming a perpetrator
in the invisible,
the improvable;

a genocide.
a geocide.

bang! 05

bang!
the material
rapidly consumes the void.
a chain reaction,
the dynamic dissects
the stagnant
pulling back the skin
peeking upon
the mechanics
being born
from an
interrupted nothingness
dust disrupted
by a object
unseen to us
as quanta
buried in such quantity.

we know only
that we have been awoken
by its wake,
the mere ripple
of its passing.

the pulses of pulsars,
heartbeats,
and galaxies dancing
arm in arm
helixing upon each other
carrying in the karyote
on the tip of my finger.

a universe from
a single touch
perhaps even mindlessly.

e=? 05

where are the atoms
and quanta?
(and all those other
specially flavored bits)

not of physical,
are the physical.
probably here
(but maybe not)
energy
the ability
to do work,
to produce change
(and a hammer
is the ability to pound
a nail into a board)
defined by a silhouette?
by a shadow
and not the form
standing against
the flicker of this fire.

what if both
science and religion
have been kneeling
in the same church
and never knew it?

(just shapes cast
upon different walls)

and all this inertia
simply a thought
not yet concluded.

lucretius 05

a 6 year old
in the living darkness
of my room
trying to imagine
what infinite was.

passing the interrupting
tree fingers,
a goodbye of letting go

i wondered if i'd float
if the world stopped spinning

and then up.

my vertigo's view
into the universe
and the clouds ripped
too easily
the more i clung
the more i was pulled
by the weight of another
sphere.

a spiritual vertigo,knowing
my body and mind
would never be set
right again,
an equilibrium
of quaking fluids
on my inner ear.

shivering in the black
behind the sky,
full of nebulae simmering
of monstrous miles
my edges glistened
in a cold numbness

and my arms spread
a panicked infant
raised suddenly to
a great height
preparing for the impact
that must follow
such impossible altitudes

and i left myself.

lucretius
lancing the night
in pajamas
a ragdoll
trusting the
unknowable.

cross pollination 05

and the strung lights
on the porch
are playing the
wind chimes
with a giddily competing
unsynchronized
on and off
reminding me
that it is summer,

and not to think
but to listen to
the whispers that the trees
are barely saying.

and squirming caterpillars
attempt to
possess the house
with their multitudes,
curved up heads
of lost wondering
over an edge
searching for the next
surface
with some instinctive
expectation,

like me,
stubborn
little terrestrials
staring down
the nemesis orbit
of an asteroid
in a distant night,
as dandelion puffs
have shattered
into an invasion
of probes riding
a summer solar wind

wishes rooting
themselves
like ticks
like an artificially
inseminated species
into earth.

"the aliens are here"

pondering my hand
long enough
makes this shape unfamiliar;

a hieroglyphic biology.

an anatomist,
i try to infer
its function
from its form,

the thick padded palms
and textured tips
to reach, to grasp
to grip

and wonder
if our hands
created our curiosity
or was it the other way around?

nymphalid 05

a butterfly flapping
my wings
hoping for an
effect
on some distant day,

that somehow
each molecule of air,
each transient strand
of wind
will carry my shape
beyond me
and that my actions
can be more
than i am
than i can ever understand.

across a sea
lapping upon
a starlit sand,

my flit and
flighting being
stirring colors in the sun,
can teach
a larger eye
than i,
fragility
and my stillness,
life

demure 05

her downward
smile
she laughed at me

in the kindest of ways,

with dimmed
demurred eyes
drawn away
so that i would
not
be humiliated
(too much)
by the fact

that she really
saw me.

even as her lips
squirmed
and tightened
against each other
in childish rebellion
against her decorum
she
shushed them
with the shake of her head
and an escaping breath
that said it all
anyway.

slow 05

it was such a
slow seduction,
that it snuck up
on both of us.

a glance,
that turned into
a conversation;

a smile,
the outstretched
in lush grasses
into a picnic;

a walk
that escalated
into a sudden
stillness

in which our eyes
darted in and out
of each other

not admitting
or alighting
to where their focus
was,

a nesting
wit all its warmth
and restless shuffling
of newborn
blind hunger

clumsily
raising our lips
for nourishment.

optivore 05

you glistened
a wet still staring
hover
among the ferns
and palms
whose fingers
held you at a predatory
distance from me.

after all
it was your eyes
that were feeding,

their pupils learning
ingesting with their
swallowed widening,
my every
instinctive procedure;
the stillness that started
at every
sudden stopping
of footfall
and its beginning again.

the scent of my sweat
an emission
my pores, pouring
this sea of fear.

even as i was
already being consumed
by the taut curiosity
in your face
and the precise way
your nose inched
and followed me
when i felt safe enough
in my aloneness.

incomparable 05

all this defensive fury
frostbite
to that which dares
touch me,
a cryogenic gasp
holding until
it is safe
to breathe again;

the prayer
of an agnostic
with an atheists reverence
and a supplicants doubt.

and still all parables
are incomparable
to what the truth
must be.

i place
my hand upon your chest
to somehow
reset myself
to the rhythm there,
a penetrating voice
just below my perception.

my lips pressing
upon your temple,
here
i found a place
to worship.

mute 05

a banshee
screaming with a whisper
a revenge curled
upon a murderers ear,

an unspent shriek
of crouching needless
insanities,

my eyes emit
a faceless source
of ocean
carving away the
landscape of my profile
making me
a voiceless sphinx
stripped of my last
texture
eroded by a long
forgotten rain,
my curses
threaten to splinter
my teeth
with their unsaid.

the telephone
is mute with
my anger
and the clock
knows how much
time i have wasted.

coming 05

i've tried all manner
of lubrication
to loosen
this elucidation
but all that
comes

is a slow constricted
hiss of expulsion,
an anti-explosion.
debris
of oxidized extraneii
now free without
the function
of their other parts
and hinges,
the twinges
came

and spun, spiraled
rusted larvae
in an afterbirth
of clockwork parts
geared and coiled
but never springing

all my machinations
working for a time
that never
arrived.

habit 05

i want to stop
and fade
into the shadow
of this tree

but headlights
keep illuminating,
enlightening me
plucking me
from this pity
and i wipe off
the glisten
from my face,
the salt that will
only draw more
predatory shadows,

while passing giggles
with holding hands
find a way
to make beauty

enrage me.

earlier you had asked
how my lips
could be so still,
how could i envelope
and never bring myself
to being read.

"habit"

instead
i find warmth
in a coffee cup,
company
in conversations
with myself

and an uneasy truce
in all the things
i cannot control.

a wake 05

the ocean tide
cascades
over my mind,
tickling my nerve endings
coaxing them to rise
just above the surface
to sense the cold air,
to shiver in the sun,
while the depths
hold my lids shut
with their heavy,
with their hypnotic night.

sound is the muffle
of distant fish
schooling my ear,
touch is dissolving
into foam
and debris for
minute predators.

my breath
is drowning
without the reflexive
struggle for life.
it is drinking.

the moon is swaying me
a mother to my skin
marinated in sweet salts
adapting me to this sea
that brings all
senses and silences
to me
in currents
to my floating place

until some distant quake
reverberates
and my eyes
scorch in waking upon
the air
all knowings
evaporate,

and all my descriptions
are simply
using one dream
to explain another.

man's world 05

my eyes
are snap shots
of my distraction;

a gnat whizzing
from perch to perch
in streets famished
for reformation
and instead
littered with
men at work
with jackhammers
on the concrete
and all the other
phallics
who cant fuck
and talk to me
in the same the day,
and need 24 hrs
to pretend im 2 people.

love is just a form
of insecurity
that attempts
to sate itself
with cannibalism
and carnivals
carve it all
with Pygmalions.
lions
lazy in the sun
and somehow
still kings.
that royalty is a measure
of irresponsibility,
a church
of illiterate
assaults of doctrine.

a is for apple
get your own dinner
a is for atom
just another tantrum
well
b is for bitch
but not yours
c is for cunt
tired of being fucked
d is for dike
damning you
e is for eulogy
you will be your own

but that's not why
i wear black.

2 peces 05

taking shelter
in this cold
this disconcerting
concert
of the doubts.

in a calculated way,
i chase them away
with harsher truths
but my hands
are too small
to warm
all of me at once.

and there are places
they cannot reach.

but i will bathe
myself in them anyway,
fossil
i press into
into this sound
i am stretching,

peaces

i spill into
my form
a scorched shadow
of a fallen star
a cataclysm
a catechism
of twitches
and near dead
noise in spasm
on the floor.

"someone!?"
get a doctor
let's finish her sooner

shape me
until i am small
rape me
until i am hollow

a china box
for all those
implacable,
unplaceable

pieces.

myopia 05

and i am trying
to enjoy
these days
before destruction
wondering which form
it will take.

but there was
just a second,

just there,

where i stepped
into a future without bounds,
an old world navigator
sailing off the edge
of flat earth.

born insight,
from sight,
and was not consumed
by taxonomical atrocities
or the blue ocean
but where
traveling this sphere,
a azure line
kept itself before me

possibly promising land
but at least
guaranteeing more sky

an unafraid breath
that just may bring another.

is all this a wake,
a funeral,
or a leviathan passing
reverberant of the already
resolved, dissolving
into this foam
and then into
the stillness of the horizon

is one
just 0 + 1?

and all our sanctuaries,
pleasantries
to make this passing
a passage
we would willingly
walk through.

the fog is coming close
again
and my pure-view
purview
shrinks with this
myopia.

stranger 05

walking a desolation
of road

mother and infant
she drives by.
i reach into my pocket.

her eyes widen
with fear,

at my hand,
at what my thoughts
and fingers
might hold,

that random catastrophe
just may have
finally found her,

kidnapped like
all those she was so sure
had done something
to provoke it.

it is a slow second
her terror,
my amusement.

my hand
around texture
and leather bound

i pull out my notebook.

arrest room 05

slurping down
the black
she traded for sunshine,
she greeted people
like nazis
just to taint
the courtesy
with a more honest
servitude
and over running sinks
singed with phosphorescence

the girls
squawk, peck
preening
at their perfect plumage
careening
flittering with glitter
fitter-than fantasy
blonde head first
into mirrors
and other alluring
reflective surfaces.

except these swallows
restrain their gags
and reset
their strained, broken necks

with another stiffening

and set
all manners of tourniquets
for the bleeding
the injury
and the seeding
they were born for
with all their breeding.

trans-mute 05

the realization
that registers
as a raw signal
at a nerve
ending, arriving
uninterpretable
by the brain,
that in some
feralautistic mode
of analysis
catalogs every curve
as it disrupts
other traveling impulses,
and stimulating others
that arrive in long dark
wildernesses in which
they are, at first,
lanterns

inwardly illuminating,
in worms and reprograms
as you find worlds
in a rotted woodknot,
faces in the shadow
of a brittle wallpaper;
rewriting all your
booleans, loopholes
and backdoors

and what all your beliefs
mercifully told you not to think.

a bubble collapses
into the other side
of your previous
universe.

death valley 05

amnesia.
in the desert.
how did i get here

to the lowest point ?

just searing and
sand trails
of unfamiliar creatures
now shading themselves
in the leewards
of brittle branches
and shards
of ancient pottery
that were once
a salvation for water
but deliver only dust
to my lips.

am i drying up?
will this book
have an ending
in white empty pages
a record
of all dwindlings
bleached by this sun
and blinding me

or have age and trauma
hybridized a horrible
maturity
where muteness
is the local dialect?

is that why
only lunatics
hear god talking to them

wandering the wastelands
and talking only
to themselves?

higher ground 05

i am traveling
the bell curve again
and it is a very
sharp turn to
down,

and those on higher ground,
unaware that the water is
rising

it is the simple
and the brilliant
that will drown first,
on this hill
while
i am strung up
by the rain
and hanging
white knuckled
on the electrical wires
for a signal

to make me a conductor
or
shock open my grip
and send me
falling too

gurgling and gasping
in the inches
my life will be
measured by.

decoherence 05

the night is jeweled
with the sea creatures
floating within it.
each radiance
splaying with a near
physical brilliance,
glittering upon
the rain dancing,
across my forehead
as if it suddenly has
other places to go.

my skin
is too saturated
with clarity
for it to cling to me,
swimming
in all this air
that a coming front
has stirred up.

my hair
curls in its eddies,
a dynamic edifice
of da vincian turbulence
carefully crafted
from chaos, forcing
every pore
open and breathing,
all exhaling at once
having been long closed
in a heightened protection.

i am strangely
attracted

to this disorder,
to what it dissolves
and reassembles
even as it
no longer resembles
me

and i refuse
to be reformed,

preferring
this dissolution
to any other
solution.

fragmented
this broken down
element
has more reaction.

wigner's friend   05

a sound processing
as shape
and manifesting
as being,

the music
of that first plucked string
of creation
smoldered like coals;
the voice it whispered
deliberately said nothing
but a child's
senseless riddles
to travel
below my radar
and around the corners,
intending to confuse
anything logical,
to make it diffuse
before it could find me
a callous
of a disappointed wound.

but still the
words had fingers
needful of giving to me
a sense of other
so that in my seeing
it can be;

pulling my face
to the wide of the sky,

to this landscape transpiring
expiring expirating
its breath,a pulse
expanding
the blood vessels
in my limbs,

dilating my eyes
for the smallest registering.

the quantum
plays as fireflies
and my hairs
stand in reverence
to their electricity
against the night

so i can lay
on the grass
beneath it,
until it can see me.

mr. monotony 05

why come up
with new words
for old worlds.

i could holler like a hole
and cut myself
on the edge
of your expectation

"that's life"

an attempt
to make my mouth
vestigial
and my lips
lean on each other
awaiting your wisdom
and accept that love
is mindless mannequins
rubbing against each other
in a squeaky friction,
blank stared
glazed with repetition
and emotional anatomy
that cant even summon
epicurean reverie.

i am supposed to want this?
"that's life"
i am supposed to love this?
"that's life"

feeding me a simple line,

as if i were
a device made
too poorly
or too well
for this simple
process of illusion.

regressing 05

my boston foot,
heavy on the gas,
my whims brutal
to the wheel;

a suspension
in suspense
of collapse.

anything for a bass beat
i itch
like i am trapped
in this car with
mosquitoes.
navigating tree-lined
roads
winding
scratching, swerving
staggering
the yellow line
in my ridiculous
death throes.

with highbeams
pushing me.
i pound my breaks
to make him more
hesitant.

the turn is clicking
plucked like half a symphony,
a revolutionary,
plowing down the highway
but the gas gauge
needles at my complicity,
a fashionable fanatic.

a radio
is trying to tell me
i am asleep,
humming about
room 101
and creatures
behind human faces,

simians socialized
into artificial selection
and conditioned reflexes
and a false sense
of survival
that is killing us.
regressing to all our
failing strategies
because they worked once,

or at least we
were told they did.

chimera 05

as bones
my consciousness
is crushed and reset,
so it will grow into the
mutated or become
parts lost
and long since replaced,

now conducting themselve,
now constructing themselves,
into the whisper
that answers
but my thoughts
are only hurriedly
strung together
like a child's necklace.

this ache,
its hard edges
passing
the jagged parts
on my flesh.

and the tv
provides a false company
a night light to chase
these monsters from me,
these might happens,
these should haves;

faces dulled from
luminescent silver to tin
only an obligatory glimmer
for those would oblige me
to sleep,

and thus i am an insomniac.

my eyes dried, stuck
with long wakefulness
scorched with this
flickering chimera,
this flesh
has grown around
the scar tissue
even blind fingers
hesitate upon
with remote sensing.

pulling upon a texture
never quite forgotten

as if even
skin must remember
its most lethal danger
and point of destruction
to avoid it.

sandbox 05

"what are you?"
"what i have always been,
a precocious child"

twirling your hair
around your finger,
you were flirting

with an idea
some siphoned cipher
feeding the involuntary
hum;
smiling the relief

of a deliberately
forgetful moment

that had allowed you
to remember

a sandbox universe,
strewn with toys
and nimble creeds of youth,
that was larger
than this one

"wouldn't it just
fuck
the materialists
if the unreal
was the ruler
to measure the real?"

throwing your head back
and making the ceiling
melt away
with the relaxations
of muscle
and round of eye
searching
the planetarium
of your eyelids
for stars.

salvage 05

alive
but a meshwork
of injuries,
the wrinkles on my face
are converging tides
carrying with them
what the moon
pulls from the black
with her curiosity
and leaves with
glistening alien patterns
upon this shore.

i feel a kindred complexity
as i look upon these
pristine and quiet shapes
and spoken horizon
with unbroken blue.

i am a salvage
operation and
i'm just watching
for what might
glimmer up from the
sea floor.

a sparkling
necessity
of lights,
the effervescence
of conversation
is a seashore
rupturing
upon my ears.

this luminescence
is casting shadows;
the reality
i realize
a deluge
so much part
of the same ocean,

a wave following another,

tumbling, tearing
through the rupture.

vicarious world 05

i watched
across the table.
the warmth
my company
afforded you
allowed you to uncoil,
uncurl,
so that in my eyes
you could find a
sun to grow toward
(that somehow
even your scars could
pattern with the
beautiful intelligence
of ivy)

your glances
divided about the room
part ready to venture
again, in
part expecting old threats
to flesh themselves
with new hands.

your stomach
remembered
to be afraid again,

a taut blessing
of near nausea
that let you know
this was not
my last meal

but that there will
eventually be one.

and it can happen
any time.

even as your
merely polite smiles
stumbled accidentally
into a laughter
that could forget

looking upon me,
a helpless spectator to
your worry and your want,
your eyes faded
into that never-stare
that was so convinced
the earth was no place
for such possibilities

anthesis 05

a Rorschach
is blossoming from
my eyes upon this cloth.

an inner structure
is failing.

there are still cells
of me left to collapse
my neurons
are getting a fix
off the endorphins
my fear is releasing;
the sugars feeding me
the illusion of a
temperate season.
the disconnected branches
of my nerves,
threatened
now flower words
as if at least
my voice
could travel the years
my life will not reach.

should i prune off parts
and allow panic
to make me bloom
again
again

a relenting spring
without a winter
without a fall?

fallen
these petals
are spinning on their axis
brushing each other
in passing,
in this centering
tightening my ribs

braids them (beautifully)
breaks them (brutally)

into the silence
you want from me.

endozoan 05

and i can be thankful
for
cold and rain
for the way it
wakes me,
reminds me
of my skin
and that i am
warm.

this
wants releasing
but remains clinging
to the bottom of my stomach
digging itself in,
and the loosens its grip,
a trapped parasite
sensing an exit near
because i am no longer
a gracious host
in all the things i swallow

and for once
i am feeding off of
it.

the curses that fly
from my mouth
are its protests,
its volatile offspring.
my arteries
curls and coil
around it
feeding it upon
my blood supply
(with all its toxins)

but it wriggles against
this breath of cold
so at least
i wont mistake it
for a source of
nourishment.

microscopic me 05

the unelectronic silence,
the clutter shut off
by my forgetfulness
to push a button
or click a light,

it is a thick
crackling in my ears
a glass slowly shattering.

a simple human,

not a node
at a network hub
nor a cognizant router

just me gnawing
on a fingernail
in blessed
under stimulation

wondering
each creak in the
architecture
for its origin
and comforted by
the irregular pulse.
of automobiles passing

that i was not
the last and only,
just a lone, lonely
so unused to my
own heartbeat
that i thought
it was another's footsteps.

the only prowler
in this black
is the shade of me
stretching outward
into the non-light
until even
the walls thin
and the stars stare
over my shoulder
bringing the cold
in with them.

a lens
of a larger eye
upon microscopic me.

implode 05

"what i was
could have saved us..."
she said;
she stood
a measured mash
and music
of mechanical twitches
needing to be
as numb
as a newly tempered
alloy.

she was
a series of
impossible alertness
and simultaneous distance.

fear
it made her
more precise,
a screaming face
frozen
at its own mirror glance
calmly analyzing
itself
peeling back petals
impenetrable,
as a fractal

a pattern
never escaping itself,
the further in
the further saturated
was her consciousness
a white noise
hissing from the flickering
light bulb
that her eyes pulsed to,
trying to decode its signal,
aligning her breathing to it

to the growls
of his mouth
the ever-distorting shape
of his lips,
the spasm of his face.

but it was just
an insects nerves
he's already dead...

and soon
still, still expecting

that the room
would come back

but the universe
collapsed
to a point
of light

"but you just decided
to destroy both of us..."

folded 05

an organelle
folding upon itself,
touching two thoughts
that would otherwise
never conceive
of each other,
bringing an explosion
to each universe
a devastation
that may organize
into new life;
a cell that would grow
around you.

you sat there cross legged
and crouched
a two sided
knot of not
and never
or maybe
never daring to day yes,

fearing to disturb
an already fragile
process of beginning
and ending.

that horror
maybe a more
durable weed
than hope,

or at least more prolific.

you did not
want to give it
one breath
to feed upon

gossamer 05

we are dead
and alive
as all immortal things,
tender treshed
gold and vanilla
contours
curling toward
each other.
the glow shimmering
upon the oils
of your skin,
a gossamer
that clings as
a web you are
pulling from your face.

our breaths
communicating.
a child's
upward curve of nose
slicing the air
innocently nuzzling
upon the scent
of my sensing you,

careful not
to put words to it

just smiles
and artfully
glistening eyes.

perhaps 05

I've never seen
the tide so low

is the world ending?
are the oceans
receding
like all the secret
pentagon memos said?

perhaps the news reports
announced it one night
while i was stoned
with the zeal
of forgetting
or
growling to the wall
of my self pity,
all the words
ricocheting back at me.

was i the last to know?
are all these people
just going quietly?

perhaps doing
what they have always done
weekday coffee,
afternoon commute,
strolling upon
these boardwalks,
collecting the details
of each others faces
and the warmth
of clasped hands
a last time;
finally free
in helplessness.

or perhaps it's happening
so slowly
that to mortal eyes
it is just a change
in the tide

mad-wry-gal 05

she wails a sequence
of numbers,
a skipping calliope
and a mistuned piano
that could be
the beginning
of a sweat softened, torn
piece of phone dialup lie
or the half swallowed
realization
of a bill she cannot afford;
trying to wash it down
with repetition,
a method of
childish distancing,
that if she tosses
them out into the
air enough
the acrobatic tumblers
will rearrange them
into a figure
to fill the doorway
with the contour
of a companion
she could
count upon.

entrance 05

you smiled
an iconoclast
smashing
all the sacred jars
and defacing
all my featureless beliefs,

turning over
every mossy rock,
peeking between my papers
an unattended child
just wanting to see
my secrets
without the presence
of parental eyes.

humming
in deliberately wordless
grasping
upon the air
pulling each note
strumming
with drowsy fingers
just enough
beneath my skin
to be
too close,

orchestrating
the incandescence
and cadence
of your eyes
to sway with candlelit wind.

as i
gratefully searched
these glimmerings
for an entrance,
entranced
by the rustlings from
within
endangering me
with a surrounding
side-glance upon me

and sunlit window
within them

illuminating in my
direction
absorbing me
until i am completely
within you.

comet 05

sky a nuclear
cotton candy

back illuminated
night of trees,
a near obscene
green on pink
softened by a violet

taos hums
while lunatics rock
themselves
in time with their
self serving lullabies,
the earth spinning,
children in the tide
of a mothers breathing
praying for cataclysm
to promise that change
will not be put off
completely.
convinced
that thunder is God.

while in my quiet
this fear is a
scent sparkling
on the edges of the air
scaling my face
with insectile gentle
travelings
shivering each minute hair;
knowing
there are levels to order
we will never understand,

but there is
a human level;
a constant grist
pearling upon
this pain.

in a nudge of massive
subconscious will
the human race
is inviting a comet
in a fit of self loathing
of suicide that upon
a glint, a streak
against the black
too bright and too close to
be a star
they will finally
wish for anything else

lazuline 05

i am writing these songs
for the end
like it is the beginning,

and all tomorrows
are enough to outlast me.
this blue sky,
a taut bed-sheet, stretched
just an hour passed
my dying, dimming retina,
protects its last projection.

forever lazy beneath lazulline,

sweating away
my consciousness
to a reactive yellow radiance
slowly exploding through time,
that in creating me
has dibs on my destruction.
(though my own kind
will no doubt claim me first)

all the promise i need,
to sleep on
such sweet grasses,

an alp to an ant,
a mite to a mountain

and mattering to neither.

my smallness
and mortality
promise
this permanence.

vox 05

words
like paper
randomly ripping
into an exquisite pattern,
you threw out
your voice
into me
to hear an echo
from
each concave,
each enclave,
traveling
all remote
untrod floors
and untried doors,
expanses
of black hallways
each
a territory
with its own language,

all answering
with a skip
in the count
of my breaths.

my lungs panicked
and reset
with a few shallow sighs,
while all other parts
of me
struggled for a silence
i found only
in the open of sky
from my windows,
awaiting
those conversations
only finished years later.

a communication
the light of stars
delayed,
the measure of our
distances,
until we are only hearing
each others pasts.

goldilocks zone 05

the pavement
feels soft
with the comfort
of gravity.

i can sleep
now
that i am awake
and dream
now
that i know the real

is make-believe.

and with the sun comes
exposure,a searing
of this naked skin

and the heat
of the star
is just far and gentle
enough
not to scorch
all this green.

but all of my layers
it burns away
the epithelials
of an older me
while the air
i breathe makes
a slow bonfire of me
from within.

and i am wondering
this morning
about all the moments
up until this one:
the progeny and the pruned.

a buddha
smiles in a storefront
its quiet face waiting
for me to look upon it.

should i simply pack
and drive away
leaving it
to stare after me?

are these paths
the indistinguishable
folds of a flower
so much upon themselves
that i cannot see
where one choice
ends and the next begins
except for the merciful
destruction between
it grows from?

sometimes
a hard morning
can make for
a beautiful afternoon.

window 05

dawn,
rupturing of sun
across the sky
from its distant
distorted
place in the black,
pulling from me
with its gravity
my shrouded atmospheres.

if all
i need is a little denial,
then ill do that.
if i need
a little realization
then ill do that too.
a bit apart,
so its that much
easier to see
these what-ifs
and why-nots.

if sleeping is opaque
and waking is translucence
then i am still
a window
neither inside nor outside
in some in between
that sees something
of everything
but understands nothing.

the world travels
well into shadows,
in flight
across my surface
where i can sense the
edges
but not touch them
and the colors
are still veiled from me;
a scratching
on a outer door,
a curling
of repetitive motion
of habit,
an exhale
would be had
without me
and i'm left
to wonder again.

am i
a wind or a ghost
merely moving behind a
curtain?

ambushed 05

so carefully clasping
veins and flesh.
why am i here
to be so separated?

why my lungs insist,
why cry, why ears exist
if there is nothing to say.

and there is a dilation
just behind my ribs
and just in front of
this injury
expanding,
pushing aside
all other organs
into my throat
behind my eyes
nurturing a rage
that only feeds itself
more hunger.

i attempt to release it,
a rifle set against
such a delicate
form of bone
wrapped in flesh
somehow housing
that which has
yet to be proven, but more
palpable than pulse.

its not the dying,

it's the gradations
between,
the floating moments
where there is an alien
in the mirror
more real than
this skin bound for death
and doing anything
to avoid it.

but ,waist deep,

i am ambushed
by the parts of me
submerged, praying
for a finger twitch
or
for the tide to rise
and take me completely.

blasphemer 05

you have to believe
to blaspheme

and know it was a lie.

it will take time
to shell this grief,
this remnant
fitting a series
of prosthesis,

a box of shattered pieces,
a rattling
of jarred gears
broken of function.

but
my doubt has made me
more devout
and my fear has made me
more ready;
a bowl waiting for a meal,
a curvature craving an echo.
my lungs
signal my primitive brain
for a breath of air
heavy with information
to translate into either
silence or words
to speak for the
phantom ache
between
my throat and stomach
cutting itself from me;

separating to survive.

and i am wondering
about all the people
who are not here
and all the ways
they are not.

differential 05

each variable
i replace always
amounts to
me equalling 0.

every faith
negates itself
with its actual practice.
each love is null
in its requirement
that i be everything,

except me

in this place of rage
and insurmountable fear
i pause
upon my reflection,
i lean in prayer
against a mirror,
too close
to see myself.
as if unfocusing my eyes
could blur
the edges of this sense
of self, of other
and i grin
waiting for a feedback
to make it sincere
but its only the
same old grinding.

if it wasnt for smiling
i would find
something more horrible
to do with my teeth

like snapping
or gnawing
at my own wrists
for escape.
instead
all i manage
is a fierce giggle.

should i invest
in roller blades
or razor blades?

either
is a clean solution.

.... . .-.. .-.. --- 05

exiles in silences
watching the streams
behind each others eyes,

as my nervous twitches
encoded in dots and dashes,
shallow breaths
and flicking lashes,
my want for escape
from this dull little prison
of human flesh.

screaming in communiqués
in my tapping foot
hoping that some
fellow-trapped
will decode them
or at least send
one back
cutting the sludge
of all these polite
exchanges;
these words whose noise
changes
nothing, but lay bare
all with a dissection
that kills
every specimen.

but our spasms
spoke to each other
without our knowing,
seizures seizing
the opportune.

father 01

he looked around the room
for something to offer her
but more to break
the gaze
that unflinchingly absorbed him.

this acceptance
he was not used to.

such eyes
were so usually purchased
so casually bartered with
not offered so freely.

and their expanse
was sky
seen from the other side
the fragile orbs
hung as tender planets
before his star,
but he felt as void
with a
wounding gratitude
for their glowing surfaces.

he wondered
if whatever it was
that was god

simply created
out of loneliness
for a purpose,
for another
set of eyes
to look into.

he wondered
if it had felt
as humbled as
he did now
when another hand
reached so helplessly
up to him.

and had it looked
away
and was still searching
for something to offer.

he would let god search.

he would look back
into his daughter's eyes

the empath II 01

and she turned
some soft flesh
within her, bleeding.

her eyes the downcast veil
as if closing off a portal
to an abyss
she had grown
to know as lover,

that she could
condemn no one else to.

for she would not feed
greedy upon concerned eyes
as teeth and claws
that hovered
invisible, but sensed,

between human bodies
between infant and breast,
between the sighs

and short lived intensities
upon breath in private ears;

the voices of need.

and she stood
stillness aspiring to become
silence
so the need in his eyes
would pass her unnoticed.

so much attention
and it left her unattended.

hands, eyes
with practiced tenderness
attempted to infuse her
by refusing her.

the room
expanded and contracted
with the pulse of waiting.

she folded her arms
and felt the only
embrace she needed.

meat
12.30|01.24.06

I no longer have dreams,
I have nightmares
with eyes.
no longer with a kind,
I feel no kindness.

what you call divine
has cast
and cast me away.

now is a world of
lecherous, raping hands
smug, sociopathic smiles
and feet
of a marching machinery
that will grind my bones
into the barren mulch
that once was jews
and lynched niggers.

I am alone,
all species are dead to me
and I never existed
to my own.

no god, no devil
only earth
has rights upon this corpse
when these butchers
are through
mutilating it.

this is not flesh
I was never anything

more than meat.

bigot 06

my 8 cylinder
road tearing
wife battery
ocean raping, oblivious
to all that applies
to anyone but me--
those
niggersimmigrantsfaggots&cunts
should know
that the world is mine.

mine mine mine.

I built it on their
bloody, splintering,
tectonic backs
and I scream injustice
if they shift
into the smallest quake,
rippling
my seamless unseemly.

lets go back
when girls were too illiterate
to know what rape meant.
(or at least to testify)

when the nobility of suffering
was a social calling.
(for those I wanted to underpay)

and all my atrocities
were whispered euphemisms.

lets strip it all back.

after all,
my name isn't Niemoeller
and I don't even know
who he is
(besides all those jews
had it coming--
they should've just
somehow
known)

because history
hurts everyone

else.

inbetween 06

this place
of many borders,
of sun and nigh,t
of sky and sea,
of sand;

of the infinite
length of edges
as their ends meet,

this is home
the inbetween
and the outside.

and the fog is blocking
the horizon from me
and bringing it
to my feet
like a frail quiet servant.

I am a creature
with no religion.

belief is just
a willingness to lie
about what you
cannot admit;
replacing it
with the unreachable
that will never
cut your fingers.

I am
without
continuity,
without context
all those words
lingering in buried jars,
an edited divinity

a pregnant goddess
left upon a shore,
the world will know
only
my echo
but i will wake
all the insomniacs
on all sides of ocean.

words of rivers between
rocks,
fingers raw in digging
for cups to drink them from,

only
the mad,
the poets
& the suicides
see my face
in a rippling moon
and
my death
in their life.

bled 06

the pressing
upon her throat,
the escape
that would never happen.

only a slow
easily ignorable gasp
would replace it.

she was drunk
upon despair
wrestling her consciousness
from the light and the cold.
the dark
was at least a close warm
as the blanket
pinning her limbs
in the bruiseless way
that no lovers ever do.

her breaths
were panicked crowds
at a fire door
trampling upon each other,
all civilization forgotten.

the ache in her abdomen
and just below
reminded her,
(now and monthly)

how below
human concern she was,
bleeding
but it was
still less a wound
than her eyes
whose only use
seem to be
to see
all the ways
she wasn't human.

the regulars 06

my whys
are finding all my hollows
and my yesses
are too few.
I am the shadow
in the corner,
the meander
that predators
clutch from
the periphery.

but it only makes these
beer swilling shadows
look at me from
the sides of their eyes
at my scribbling,
at my solitary,
cautious
about all that they do not know
about me,

but I am cautious
about what
I know
about them.

a gray bearded
adolescent
wooing a waitress
with his unforgotten youth.

a cluster
of desert bleached bones
cackling
beneath sunglasses
and a wicker hat;
about Jim,
about Janis,
about how his back
hasn't known any other bed
but earth
for 40 years.

two crones competing
for a fool,
smoothing their feathers
raising their hackles
with hairspray
and twirling they fingers
through it.

and ceiling fans
sway lights,
ambered with age
and cigarettes,
in already drunken rhythms
to hypnotize
those present
from their past
with the promise
of liberation
at the price
of libation.

and like everyone else
I order
amnesia
on the rocks.

lydia 06

barefoot in a black dress,
drunk with spotlight
filtering through
the pink canopy
of her closed eyes,
an orgasm
crawling under her lids
searching for escape
at the ends of her lashes,
fluttering.

and instead
releases
a belt of voice
that whips the skins
of those standing
too close.

they fall back
but line up again
for another,
lashing the air
with a child's unceasing
repetition.

fingers groping
the strings,
as an amorous
blind man at a blouse,

while the room shakes
with seismic joy
making
the rooted and
the concrete
dance enraptured
while the timbers groan
from the release
of their long stillness.

white supernovas
ensnared in bulbs,
fireflies in jars
choose with their cadence,
which moments
to illuminate,

such twilights and dusks
allows her to see
the heaviness of air
as if the moon
was displacing the sun
and packing the atmosphere
closer to her skin;
thickening her breaths,
slowing her thoughts
congealing this clumsiness
of consciousness
into a precise residual
of all previous heartbeats

while these new ones
fall through her
and earth,
a fresh dusting
of neutrinos.
pulling her into some fetal.

her words standing nude
with stone faces
among writhing limbs
hoping to hold this season
for the rest of the year.

specimen 06

whenever I think,
I can only think
of dying,

all the fractures
and the scar tissue
tied and twisted
sinew
are braided about
the same mortal spot.

a specimen
divided by cold glass,
I can no long feel
but only look
passively upon
the stain of me
a separated sliver,
a cross-section
of consciousness.

but under
your gaze I shiver
and find corners
in open air,
in the fold of my arms
and in
side glance distractions,

an immune assault
upon a foreign entity.

your barely smile
and unflinching gleam
of eye
fixated upon mine
looking elsewhere.

an echo
mirroring its own
aphonic rustle
in its dish-eyed burrows
only to find
the inner of me
this cavity
with the skin
of the remembered.

I can't 06

this day,
this groan,
we are all monsters
or monsters hands.

while the sun
from the other side
of sea
comforts and cooks me.

I close my throat
and block my ears
to mute all sounds

I can't
breathe
I can't
be here

but it is
the without words
that makes me
wheeze on the only
available poison,
a gasping fish

I can't
be her
I can't
be

I can't

shivering in the ice
of this open
barely enough
to keep my lungs
expanded.

I can't
I can't
I can't

be an accomplice

to what we would
hide
beneath this ocean
and I can't
be anywhere else
I cant
drink
from these same
bloodied, muddied
waters

leaving me 06

among all this
dew and dimness
where my still lips
do not tell anyone
where I am,

my form
does not displace
the air, its atoms
ringing ripples
of my presence
to surfaces curious
about me
in others senses;

but swaddle me
in humid humanity
from all such spaces.

the clouds cover
the sunlight that seeks
to wake my lips,
still drunk
with blankets
and blind with
flickering lives
that murmured meaningless
illuminated scripts
to my sleeping mind.

that glisten
like all those dreams
that are not mine.

only my stomach
threatens me
with its waiting growl,
still now
satisfying itself with
the marrow of
the empty filling it.

I feed it upon
regularity and habit
while the calamity
of soon worlds
yet coming, accumulate
on all my inner edges
feeding all my doubts
their expected meal,

but for now
are not feeding
upon me.

and all these
perpetual peripherals
are gone

leaving me.

real-eyes 06

the light
sparkled through the trees,
lit birds,
and fell upon her face;
suns attempt
at the softness
of snow.
it played about
her mouth
a candied intangible,
erratic intelligence
that wanted to melt
upon her tongue.

but she was consuming
with her eyes
these swallows

of whole skies
with no holy reasons,
as if books
could validate
the brilliant butterflies
now vying
for her pupil
to learn what seeing was
when it saw beyond

their glowing,
a constellation of awe
that guided her fingers
through the air
trying to catch
the wingless
when it was already
netted
in the tangle
of the endorphin drenched
vines of their creation,

and those precociously
close
were ensnared by her
lashes
as they fluttered
into the sleep
to be the stars
on the retina
of a dream.

breakdown 06

her eyes became
rounder and dimmer
slipping, sinking
inward
as if only these muscles
had the presence of mind
to recoil
while the rest froze
in a primordial
instinct of self-defense.
they pulled in;
mammals after
a mass extinction;
deep into burrowed labyrinths
waiting for the earth
to stop shaking,

and all he had done
was grab her
hand.

but the trembling
wouldn't stop.
even
the moon shivers
still.

"I am not a person
just a history
of learned reflexes"

all twitching, flinching,
her lips moved
with a conversation
that never parted
her lips

her eyes
refocused on the t.v.
pitying the image
of a mother gone mad
at a son's death.

she always had to watch this
part

the breakdown.
when insanity
is the only sensible
response

every neuron firing,
every repressed impulse
that had remained
unacted
for mommy and daddy,
for judge and jury,
fuck them.
fuck it all.
fuck god.

let there be chaos.
let there be night.

let's decorate the room
with shards of murdered
hummels
and the ripped hems
of civilized living.
let all the tendons uncoil,
snap and seizure
and make bloodied talc
of the good china.
she watched with a pity
she could not have
for herself
and a mercy
she could not manage
for him.

she kept watching.
she kept her fists down.
she kept.
he kept
watching her.

he loved her so much
she wanted to shatter him

at the shore
the waves rippled
all   **about me 06**

I walked alone
and in
every doorway
every glance
of conversation was
all

in every sign
each glowing letter
each word a sequence
an answer
stretched out in miles
I had barely ask for
but spoken
in every thought

my skin it wraps

my will it wanders

the sky it falls
all

each eye ached and arched
eyebrows raised
wondering just what it is

they do not understand
but still know more

than I

it 06

she held
her hand
to
just between her eyes
and a little above,

to feel its shape,
just beneath
her skin

its breathing,
its relentless resistance,
its home
nestled and nested
in each crumbled nerve
tightening
gasping out
a last flash
of executed burst.
a former time
a former place
a form of her.

whose passing
went unnoticed
and she
was left
a mourner

with a hard
at her throat
refused at her mouth
but escaped
in the weakness
of her eyes
cupped there
and coaxed back
with a blinking
with a systematic
unthinking
tricked with a breath
that might just
let it be a word

and then
let it go

concerned 06

"my dear. . ."

my hand
and all the softness
there
lies to your fingers
with their uncutting;
all your kindness
only molests me
with your hands
refusing my wrists
release
to scream
to tear you open
the way
you're doing to me
now

unknowingly

and I close
my eyes, my mouth,
my need for air,
until all these itches
at my arteries
stop murmuring
for me to open them
with the dull thump
of their syllables
inside my ear.

"anything I can. . ."

"no

thank you.
this is

permanent."

tip 06

this waitress
sneers at me,
my indecision,
my small order;
sans cinnamon,
my meager coffee
for me, for my
pen
has awoken
and needs the company
of clutter, of clashes
of unleashed colloquials
and loose snippets of laughter
that fly and flutter
still half-lit ash
of a fire
that collide mid-flight
and fall light
and recrystallized
onto my ears
melting on the paper.
the tip of my pen
attempting to trace them
before they are gone

a catastrophe
of thick glass and water
jars me from the hum,
and spreads,
polyurethaning
the dull counter
with its purity

she stops
she sighs
she breathes and decides
that if they wanted perfect
they'd pay her more

she raises her eyebrows
and pretends it's all part
of the act

"would you like more
coffee?"

she pours
some more

refill repeat

in all
it barely stops the hour
for half a clock tick

then its off to the next
order
complaint
undercooked
refill repeat

she just earned
her tip.

86

underground 06

where is the next
underground?

hidden from all the
billboards and GPSs
and cells
that squawk and advertise.

where are the poets
babbling to themselves
now
beyond barcodes
that squeal and burp
like gluttonous babies
for every bit about you
written in the modern
fingerprint in 0s and 1s

where does this train
not reach

in black hums
at the end of the line
and ipods
are not plugging
the ears
stuffingandslamming
the thoughts
of the dull-eyed
into a manageable mash
but throw-back
mutations make mouths
for speaking again

where someone on this train
will look me straight
in the eye.

and children 's
stomps and babbles
translate into tomorrows
and not new
corpses for the oil trade

and kisses burn
and numb each other
and flesh hips
with scarred skin
speak as wordless and holy
as rosettaless hieroglyphs
and the raucous
and the rash spill
into rainy streets
splashing puddles
of brilliant portals

now, no foot ripples
now, no voice travels
but in steep trajectories
that crack their teeth
and skin their jaws
on the pavement
in mighty crashes

and yet there is no echo,
not a sound,
from
underground.

insurgent 06

I have come
into this world
to bend all the coffee spoons,

to make all the sighs
into breaths
of pronouncement

and to run all the
beemers & hummers
of the road
with my erratic driving.

a rainless monsoon
too soon,
watching from the window
I am
counting all
the dead turtles
on their backs
collapsed worlds

and this
oxygen deprived
exhale
is an answer
to my fainting fear.

the horizons
are closing in
with a storm
at every front

but
the fault
is all behind us

what are we going
to do
when they fill the sky
with soundless thunder
and frozen lightning
waiting at the back patio
to be let in.

its billow and bellow
the sky yellow
with the bile
that has left residence
in our overflowing veins,

as the rebels rally
the drums
to synchronize
all the heartbeats
to continue the words
of martyrs' lips.

line up,
chest to barrel,
either way
these hearts
will explode

cassandra 06

my eyes are burning
with all that has come true
and my heart is ice
with all that might

and what might does

all our burrows
are full of water
all my fears,
small animals scampering
before my car
causing my wheel
to swerve.

their eyes glowing
constellating a new night sky
all their stars
and small explosions;
their gravity
finding a place
to pull at me

but night is nothing
both waking and sleep
are dreamless
my feet feel
there are no longer
days ahead of them
to step upon

so I drive

and hope that my speeds
outrun these clawed things
and that earth
will loosen its pull on me
and I will spin
into the sky
into another sleep
that won't force
me to know
the black of waking

but my radials
are worthy
my mortal needs
automatic
and all my reflexes
preserve me

expiration 06

her breath
was rhythmic protest
against the wall.
a forced continuity,
a way of attaching
one second to the next
until she could connect
enough minutes
enough hours
to forget passed this
to collect
enough interim silences
to insulate her
from the edges
of this air
of this now
that was always there

that kept all these parts
tethered and floating
these strings knotting

that just one cut
would release
them all

and all that she was
would disperse
dissolve
a leafs escape in
random erratics
on the whispering edges
of a single wind.

and she breathed
again

who am I   06

who am I
a thump a pulse
a symphonic
now interrupted
by an unthinking
blink
of hallowed distraction
who am i
bone
warming itself
with flesh;
dressing itself
in wires
with raw disconnected ends
flailing hissing
snakes
with currents at
the curvature
of their spines
who am i
who am i
who am
eye
with which a star
can see the darkness
the infinite
can know end
and immortals , death

a wound and a womb
that will reproduce
another
who am i

in all the streets
with all these lips
the oculars ogle
upward
all the fires
warming the black
that will devour them

their awe,
their awful
all impossible light

asking with an answer,
who am i

us 06

I remember
flying through the night
with you
a headlight,
a cigarette streak;
our hair
knotting into each other
as the forced wind
of speed
invaded the open windows
frantically finding
the interior curves
like a trapped insect.

each turn
daring and disbelieving
our mortalities
as if our
combined lives
could hold death off
twice as long

maybe so long
that it would forget us.

the sky tore upon
our laughter

our turbulence
displaced stars
into a new pattern
of night.

our wake had passed
and was never coming

for us

icu 06

he had waited
all night
in a teetering universe
at the corner of
the bed
watching how the tiles
intersected each other.
at every eye-fall
his thought
traveling the same
line
to the breathing
half muffled in the pillow.

now

stirring
a hatching, stretching
its small toes
into his fleshy back
its voice
the rapturous rasp
of a forest
creeping up behind him.

he felt
her stare at him,
a left over residue of worry
still staring at
what could have --
and then shaking
it away
with a nod and will.

the cold exposure
of his neck
suddenly had shelter
curling from all sides
her hair,
a grass growing
over an impact scar
its fingers flattening
the worried lines
tied to his eyes.

and quietly
they passed a plate
to each other
in their alternating hungers :

her white skin
and glittering eyes
feeding all his traumas
the comforts
he never knew

and his finally
released sigh
all the concern
she never
knew existed.

a spec[t] 06

in faceted illumination
this sugared shore
blinded me
each small piercing glare
found correspondence
in a standing hair
and the nerve coiled there
finding its way
into my memories

and they were all
small
minutia magnified
in the complex reflex
that is me

did,
did not happen
will,
will not.

even the roar of ocean
startled by soil
is only an engram of air
upon my ear

this me is holding this
spot for the next me
to arrive
in a limited sequence
but me
now knows this
sun and me
have existed
for at least this
eternity.

my stop 06

take a breath

and then again
what's worse
than the thump
thickening
in your neck
is that it can

stop

there's worse
there's worse
there's

just no telling.
where this train
will take me beyond its

stops

and the silences
are building up
all the mouths
are insulating themselves
and crowding the
molecules out
with their unsaid

and the train filling
while the only
person speaking
is the annoying
business woman
on the cell phone
slowly releasing
a steady stream
of alternating
uh-huhs
isees
and
small laughs.

I wonder
do both
sides of conversation
sound like that,

acknowledging
but saying nothing.

stop

swish slide
and more enter
a cross section
of derelicts and debutants
with shopping bags
and sandals,
mp3 cocoons,
easily read books
and headphones
that brought along
a handsome Cuban
for company

but still not a word
but that jabbering
cell

the neighborhoods
slink by
just as sleepily
as me

"next stop
JFK/UMASS"

now a hint
of Chinese
spices the air
with exotic unfamiliarity
for all I know
he could be reading
the phone book.

but still the jabber
as the train strips
the rails with screams
and sparks with each turn
and the compartments
collide
like a lightly thumbed drum
an embryonic
percussion of heart
dragging all this life
within it.

this is my

stop

ground zero 06

the trees
are withering winds
materializing
and communicating
underground

while ive been sitting
listening for philosophy,
spoken and hidden,
waiting
for the learning curve
to straighten out.
but I am
a fuse of
confused roots.

the robins are concrete
they spill and split,
meteors,
burning in the atmosphere
of my fury
of my fleeing

I wonder
if my soul
has already escaped
through my wasted words
as we
under sun and star
think them cut from a cloth
of swaddling night;
from a bang still unfolding
a drummers fingers
trying to wake me
as I schedule my vacations
to coincide with cataclysm
hoping ill be sipping
a martini
at ground zero.

but now I hear
an Anasazi
moaning to recall me
to their memory
when they had to hide
from the sky.

and there is
no cave deep,
no cliff high
enough.

it has us surrounded.

swarm 06

a pop
a crack
a spark
the sulfur of the match
a small piece
of brimstone
to this minor
revelation

sucking the smoke
drawing into my lungs
to replace
to release
the fearful breath
caught within me;
thawing the ice left
there
by the thoughts
I scattered away,
mosquitoes
that I know
will only come
again
to draw more blood

the relentless
win
only because
they are simple
and small minded,
and deliberately focused
on their own
eventual extermination.
and because they
are many

and they swarm
again.
again.

and I exhale
dispersing them

again.

empties 06

my senses are echoes
behind my fingertips

an inner clutching
with barely attached nerves
upon an outer

as the silence
rings silver
and the house sleeps
uneasily with
already fallen footsteps
and this shivering
is the air eliminating me
through equilibrium

my thoughts are poltergeists
slamming all doors
and flickering the lights
a sporadic epileptic's insight
and illusion of movement
through time

I wonder where
all those black moments went.
seeping sand through floor-
boards
shaping what is left

our gone
have left us here
a pattern of their absence
to huddle
until our arms
become new empties

dosing 06

kissing until
my lips are a raw meat
dosed with novocain
my head half
narcotic and narcoleptic.
my hair
is wind-filled trees
tangled with
kites and sparrows
and lights trail and stretch
before my eyes,
traveling like a drunken highway
or a cigarette in a black room

twisted, used up
wrapping paper
from christmas morning
still awed at what
we uncovered,
we are still not wrapped
tightly enough
though are limbs
have somehow fused
and refused
to separate
but i cannot think
so far ahead
to wonder when
to disentangle them

we are strangling each other
to life,
waiting to capture
the souls escaping
our mouths
into each others,
preying cats at cages
unthinking of escape

lullaby 06

he hummed a tune
that reminded me
of grass and crickets
and a me that could forgive
the present moment
its imperfection
even if it perfectly
excluded me
a voyeur at its windows.
in the hushes between
each note
a breath that was thick
with forever
nourishing the emptiest ap-
petite
and slowing my pulse
a minute passed all pain.
my ears clutching upon it
pulses of wail and whisper
a cathedral of constructed
transparencies
of backward spoken prayers
bypassing the sentries
of my subconscious
with babbling,
unchallenged, untranslated
undressing me from within.
tapping their fingers
impatiently
upon my inner ear
awaking all the forgottens
that remembered me
for me
resetting all my atria

and

with a single exhale

I expose to the sun
the abyss adapted skins
of all my parasites

agnostics prayer 06

life is the foam
between the
silken saline surface
of the ocean
and its crashing
upon the shore.

between order and chaos
between two deaths
there is life.

and even if this be
a random fluctuation
and this
small self-awareness
that is you;
a transient tramp
ridings its rails
back into oblivion
it is born from,

you

are the eyes
of that cold absolute
upon itself
with immaculately imperfect
senses.
this skin,
this sight,
these ears;
the molecular transmuted
from mute
to spoken
carried with a relentless
inertia

you

can give meaning
to the meaningless,

you

can give stars
to darkness.

via 06

I am the flat.   the hard of a chair
I am the shadow.   that fights my flesh.
the shape of lights   the tea,
edges   a steaming inhale
a skin with no touch.   of esophageal fire
that
I put a prayer   with its borrowed will
of fingers to my forehead   will
as each sensed soul,   raise my voice
each unlived part of   in its eruption.
each life   this pen .
passes.   this silence.
relighting candles,   the flat of the floor
ringing recollections   that will not relent
in brass depths,   no matter
the flat of photographs   this weight.
rouses and rounds
to flesh   the sound of my voice
pinking the skin   speaking below
with a resuscitated pulse   the quiet,
coursing through these   a rupturable membrane
collapsed and empty   this small insect
with a presence   walks upon.
more alive
than my own

and suddenly
all things
are
precious

to me

outward 06

naked in the window
i looked
to find myself
in the rain
in the splashing
of bare feet
or the way the lightning
wrapped the walls
close to my skin
but
these destructions
are looking outward
at the blue
my teethe
clenching down
against the salty granule
of the sparkle
just before ocean
its taste
a memory
sunken beyond
below and bare
before me
yawning and swallowing
the sun
to douse my yesterdays
and prevent my tomorrows
from surfacing;
this half gone day
ends and begins
with each blink
and breath

expandable 06

your gaze expanded
and curved itself
outward,
a new sky
a stain glass
that meteors could not
shatter,
a blue
that could not be
asphyxiated by ash.
in its cradle
an ocean crashed
with the collective whispering
of unknowns
that grew from its bottom
brushing its inward surface
with their
almost-touching upon
the sun
and veldts were velvet
with sun-lazed species.

i lay half flattened
sprawled within
such luscious
green whispering
rain, quivering
canopies
the slivering
of leaves
anticipating
the passing of those
untrained in the night
passing over me
a dreaming mountain;
the curve of me-
a canyon,
my lazy hair--
rooting rivers

and where i did not
have to know
that the species
that i loved
considered me
as expendable
as things.

lip off 06

the rhythm of her foot
reiterated her thought.
a repeated growl
traveling with its
claws between her ears
as she watched
his mouth
awkwardly give birth
to insincerities.

die die die die die

as she swallowed
the ocean
like a Chinese brother.

its storm tides
rushing over
the levee of a tongue
she kept there.
not afraid to speak
just realizing
that there was no need.
every word would be
inherently unremarkable
not because of her mouth
but because of her lips.

silence
was her only way to prove
that he was just
talking to himself

forgotten country 06

my neck sways
upon my shoulders
with the smoke-filled
rhythms
of opium dens.
each slow rotation
of its cycle
a separate
discovered universe
each drugged mind
a one extended thought;
caravan
through the desert,
through the jungle.
walking between the waves
of each storm
it knew.

upon the dark ocean,
the frozen millennia,
a rambling lifetime,
now I can see
the size of the tsunami
that sunk me.

only now that
I walk on water--
I want to swim
but a drummer
calluses his hands
in the thunder
within and above me
demanding that I dance
as if voodoo was conjuring.

faster,

maddeningly tripping me
with its deified expectations
of my mortal limbs.
its rough, thick fingers find
my spine
and play each protuberant
bone
extracting the tone
of each hollow
empty moment
enveloped there.
some voice of myself
calling back to me
with the
syllable and semantics
of a mother tongue
of this deliberately
forgotten country.
and I its exile
docile
as the hands have been
shaping me
all along
with the echo
of each strum numbed
fingertip
in the imprint
of each footprint
behind me.

but still the sea
is hardened
beneath my feet
even as I
attempt to shatter it
with my most
forceful steps
it leaves only splinters
within the dance-thickened
flesh

of these soles;

souls
each rhythm
compressing, undressing me
until the finger pulls away
and I collapse
the string cut through each
struck with a wallowing note
that haunts the
curving corridors
of my ears
searching for a door
to enter me.

a whisper, a wind
about to raise a torrent
with a scream in me
it possesses and resurrects
this still born child
a deceased
reclaiming its birthright
from its doppelganger
my time, my turn
and the ocean allows
that I will swim again

irreparable 06

there's a consequence
for living,

dying.

these broken
cannot be

reassembled.

water heat
and all manner
of erosion
have worn them
smooth and separate
and their edges
will not meet
nor their fissures
seal,

irreparable.

only my fingers
find their places,
only my swallowed
scream
remembers
the pattern
and moment
of their fracture
and my fading certainty
of just before.

"nothing has loved me
and nothing will"

so nothing
can have me,

the only thing
the catholics and I
agree upon.

the faithless 06

pain is the skin
that must exist
on everything,
even the most
infinite love

i want to rip this organ
from my chest
its edges ache,
its limbs dig too deeply
and it feeds me
too much life
for me to live.
it doesn't allow these fingers
to numb
with its numerous warm tides;
bathing my mind
it does not let me sleep,
but sounds distant footsteps
against my slumbering drums
and forces my feet
to goosestep

over
all I know

all I must preserve
and
never speak about,
because it might wake
the sleeping.
for all those who rouse
the children
are crucified
and re-written
by those worshipping
themselves;
the faithless and the fathom-
less
with their dry lakes
and dead seas

too shallow
for life
and so steal it
from the wombs
of women mid-birth,
raptors feeding upon eggs
loving embryos
insofar as they fill
their stomachs.

these bastards,
these fatherless,
motherless

demanding mercy
from the bleeding

better paper 05

and the clouds
move rapidly
as prophecy
gathering the sun
with their storm,
pulling it
like a tide of demons
to the black
of the mountains
that make
a hastily torn edge
of the sky.

as if this,
all this,
is just
a scrap,
a forgotten footnote.

our atrocities,
aborted plots;
our holies,
half-thoughts;
and
our cataclysms,
crumplings
of a story
unfolding
elsewhere
on better paper.

newbury 06

arrogance has a brand name
and everyone is paying for it.

i have walked the stretch
of newbury
and been silently told
with each well-groomed ,
badly bred eye
that what i am becoming
is unbecoming.

i am an agnostic
reflecting upon
revelation
as cruel boys
psychologically torture
pigeons in the park
with imagined breadcrumbs
and the thunder of the
planes overhead
threaten
to shutter the
pavement.
the sun is contemplating
a cancer on my back
and the only
beautiful things
left are green
and none them have
a treasury seal.

i search for a face
seeking out mine
and get only sideward glances.
i see the invisible,
a single note fading
across time,
a thread strewn
in a careless tangle
of a world that keeps
interrupting me.

island 06

I supped
on a tangle of tides,
the salts
flared my nose
and burnt my eyes
with my
sudden submergence.

only my forehead
is surfaced
upon the cold
an island of
stars embedded
in stone
captured across the eons
stored in silica
between
the petrified
and the long passed
putrefied.

all these eternals
are limited
in my awe
in the shimmering
worship
of a salt sea;
to see
the open sky.
what the ocean
cannot
make a solution of
a dark   darker,
a deep   deeper

all my senses are
too sunken

but I feel
its breath
upon my brow

perpendicular 06

these blue
of knowing,
of directed plasma
looking deltaward,
but not downward,
and not even southward,

but from a place
perpendicular.

i am a page being read
my organs
splayed and dissected
though my skin is unbroken
my thoughts forecasting
radio waves passing stars
but in less here trajectories
with a fourth coordinate
that i can draw
analogies to
but not lines.

a square arisen,
I am reeling upsilon
but not upward,
and not even northward,

captive to another side
of this dimension.
a cross-section,
my dreams are sliced
thinly
over a higher's slide,

my terrors
are chemical broadcasts
spilled upon another's table
to be wiped away

seen as a pattern
of intelligence

or dismissed
as coincidental chaos
or the mindless panic
of a useful yeast.

animate
but mere animation
i have drawn attention
a bacterium
reciting shakespeare
to invisible eyes
i can feel upon me

noticed 06

gaze at the gods
in true form

and you shall die

or simply
be destroyed.

is that what
this is?

this lip-knotting quiet,
this concave
blocking both
breath and word
and hypnotizing
my eyes
with its
everywhere.

is that what
I did wrong?

did a truth
brush passed
one day
in a hurried anonymity
of self obsessed faces
looking at their feet,
envying
storefront mannequins
with all too white eyes
lusting
for other peoples skins
or their wallets

while i

was the only fool
to turn and look

and, even in such
ravenous seconds,

look too long

at
its huddled shoulders,
its glaring eyes
broadcasting to any taker

all too much?

is that why
we never look
at each other

too long?

or was it just
all
that unnoticing

I noticed?

letter 06

you can't but help
to listen to my words

especially
when I do not say them.

when they are
merely written
with the pigments
of sacrificed minerals,
crushed and fed
just enough rain
to stain the paper.
when they are merely
reddening your eyes
with sleeplessness
and indelible
in permanent silence
but voiced with
each glance
toward the frantic fold
you made of them
before throwing them
to the wall.

and yet they have
you
cornered.

communion 06

the air sweated
with the glisten
of dragonflies
and buzzed
with insects
seeking each others
electrical charge

upon my face
your knuckles
brushed what
your fingers
dared not touch

that such communion
was best left
to sunlight
and not
the warmth
of your hands

but to me
the air had no current
without
your presence
and day,
no light
but your skin.

pandora 06

this has a skin
this impossible form.
it did not escape
the box
with the leathered-wing
swarm
that feeds the world
its days,
but kept
one.

one sea, one blue
one grassy morning
      under silent moon,
one lazy, sweaty afternoon.
one night as crickets say
      to a firefly spark.

one you
that patiently waits
for impatience to fail.

this one,
this frail
that fractured
and became more;
each a mirror shard
a reflection with no match
but that of just before

still 06

that wide
that glisten

that last breath
that always
preceded another

that still
hysteria
that sent all
the unphysical
raving naked
in the street

when her body
had to sit,
her eyes
forgot to blink
and her hands
stopped
above her mouth
mid-prayer
mid-shriek
still deciding upon
either.

she could not
believe
the world

was happening.

indiscriminate 06

foreheads pressed
to each other
in an
osmotic communication
while their lips
flirted
with meaningless words
and brushed
when they both
said the same secret
and closing their lips
upon each
others breath.

their nerves
were backward-played
chimes
indiscriminate
from each other.

miscellanea 05

my eyes are swollen
with the lateness
and latency
of the previous night.
manifesting
in accusations
all the lunatics
come out blathering
all the terrorists,
threatening
and all my memory
will not let me forget
who i am,

when forgetting
is the only narcotic
for the sleep i need.

the universe has pulled in
all its folds
and pushed out all
manner of miscellanea
hidden there.

pre-sage 06

I fought back a nerve
too often for
it to recover.

now I am
envying the dust
of Egyptian tombs
their warmth,
their life,
their light
and the youth
of vampires
and their thirst

and yet so fearing
my mortality.

I had my chance to love
but I chose to walk roads
with leafless trees
and now the false lazarus's
are resurrecting themselves
unqualified
in their never living
and the slaves
work so much for survival,
that's all they ever do

a breath that does not
allow a pause or a word
but leads only to
the next one.
they are collecting
behind me
into a wind.

do I want to see
the omen
against the barely blue
of night sky.

if it means my end,
if it means that
all that i fear is coming.

I blink it away
with my unwilling eyes
leaving me
a rag of exhilaration
now sputtering in the storm
its torn tearing
the silhouette of immortality
that all loved things
must have.

ee 06

his quiet,
his voice
was like hearing
her name
across a crowded room,

through the chatter.

as if he screamed
but hadn't
but had spoken it
calmly
as if truly thinking
of something else.

a soothing
in this uninterrupted
inertia
inert
with its ever unfolding
underdevelopment;

muting the television
of its horror,
its denial
with its
cooking shows
and redecoraters
melting and ameliorating
her senses
of the full frontal
decisions
being made

for her,
against her.

and she swallowed
ingesting
the jest of it all
and its unjust

and breathed deeply
trying to assure herself

that at least the air
was still there
but it only pulled back
choking her.

and then another
spoke,

not from a page
but from next to her.

and he had smiled at her
about to say
again
that she was beautiful,

but she could not
tolerate his words
and
what they did not say
in the same
moment.

utopiaries 06

drink to rouse
the silence,
wake the voices
murmuring in their sleep.

smell the sun,
feel your pulse
and all other improbabilities.
a crack of pavement,
an eastern coastline.
just all infinities compacted
in portable forms of being

I am here
talk to me.

the scent of light
that I remember,
has no skin
to radiate upon
just frozen prisms
persisting beneath an ice star
no melting, no dying
only lucidity
casting shadows
and poets muted with
unceasing imagery.

change here is mutation,
hope is death.

this morning
I remember
a sweet, moldering scent
that once was happiness
but I did not know it
as it passed.

of cats and kisses
and parchment utopias.

of spilt wines and left over
morsels
of plenty
left to flies
as we argued upon
the irrelevant, reveling.

a night of rain
drowning my nose
ripples upon my eyes
sparkling streetlamps into a
celestial display.

did oblivion
make me happy
or
did mere ignorance
make me thankful.

the moon sits
carefully nestled in its hues
needling me with
the balances it holds

and how it is
that I could just
not ever be
at all

thaw² 06

splintered and translucent
you unfolded
a flowering of your own
sun
to drink from
each hair, a finger
a fabric
bare and shivering
upon this
music with the edges
of an aurora
on my skin
purging of its gray
a tempering radiance
a skin luminescent nascent
meat
and truer than these scars

your hum

it managed to creep in
where the night was
so perpetual
it found all the old
fissures to play upon
an effortless pulsating beacon
that made wind
of my fingers.
your breath fed it
a prosthetic
of sun
my winters curled
in its thaw
its wordless warmth
that lulls me from ledges
and holds ice-ages
to isolated geographies
and my nerve endings

rise to it

in drinking the sky
the hairs on my arms
straightened;
seedlings
blistering their soils
with their reaching
dreaming
of new leaves feeding.
from grasses
with shallow roots
in frozen soil
each indulging in the hope
that this passing cold
was the last ever
but knowing better

saturation 06

reality should be
measured in accordance
with sunlight

but wonder,
in water.

the rain peppers my face
with miniscule
awarenesses;
clarities
that spread and splatter
waking me
exponentially
until I am
myself again

my worry,
my skin has shivered out
and reabsorbed it,
a leaf uncurling
my arid lips
have drunk
enough to part
and speak
now there is nothing
to impart

than this indescribable

devout with disbelief
the puddle reminds me
that this

is mere reflection.
my heart struggling
against my flesh,
a jarred moth
panicking in these thunders
that outvoice these flutterings
of me
clinging in wet
crevices and corners
when lightning comes
enlightening
and not evaporating
with the sun

hole 06

and down the street
I growled
all my hisses and homicidals;
my white knuckles
strangling smug words,
my fingers raping whores
that would sell us all
into prostitution
for a BMW
and a string of pearls,
a rosary
they got
from being on their knees
before the unholy.

those holes
unimpaled
with concerned thought
but strung
line by line
a descension of breeders
getting duller and muter
with each succession
with each success
of properly applied
suckling

"Good girl!"
that half hearted
half year at college
taught you well

did you fuck yourself
into an appropriately
loveless marriage?

now get a blue suit
and a token job
and tell all the
minimum wagers
you share their pain
while doing your best
rip-off of Jackie-O

good little . . .

all these little girls
who dare say
what kind of woman
I should be.

if woman is all
below the waist
than I will
show you all.
not little worded
and lower case but
C - U - N -T
but I think
it's my other lips
that worry you
more.

yes I will splinter,
yes I will break
but only
under the weight
of a billion
gang banging cowards.

I am proud to break,

it means
I was
WHOLE
to begin with.

mpg 06

how many of my heartbeats
has my fear and rage stolen

I keep few days
behind me
and none of them
Ahead

just more road
just more digging
into my future poverty

just more
miles per gallon

I shriek and scratch
at the pause in traffic
all these stupid slows,

only their neurons
more lethargic,
only their philosophies
more unmoving

with all they
are supposed to love
while my hum of a
heartbeat
and drone of consciousness
swaths and swaddles me

a cocoon spun
from will

and wont

while the oblivious
thrive
drive

blonde bitch
brushing back
a hair
and any concern
for humanity
in casual contempt
while her
petroleum glutton
hums
grinding and masticating
upon dead dinosaurs
not yet knowing
she is the next extinction
the next race
of idiots
who just didn't adapt
to survive.

survivors 06

the shore had haunted
her dreams again
the sand in her eyes
stung with salt
she wiped it away
where should could picture
them both dying
in some windblown place
without sun
but his arms
but now the fog levitated
outside her window
a ghost stalking
her with blindness
mindlessly staring
though the cold,
bypassing all flesh and bone
but its haze making worlds
curled in this arch
they were saved
in the enclave
this last curve
just enough for shelter,
but still within
a skin-cell's width
of winter.
coiled to keep the cold
from passing between them
a life from their mutual deaths
and the black
encroached upon
this illumination
without light.
a dark sea
for two survivors floating
in an amnesia
of horizons
that have forgotten
skies

emergency 06

woman
all my angels
are coconspirators
in my hell
angles
on that
which would cut me

my fist flexes
reflexively
the intolerant air
is closing it
with its thickening,
its per square inch
density of dullards
slowing with the clutter
of such willing lies

trying to bend my will
by forcing my flesh

while upon a wall
of posted
christian intent
i see a list of numbers
for abuse, battery
incest

just a list of digits
for those who
hopelessly hope
but
along with us
make excuses
for those
who make the emergency
emerge

who make it
tradition

uncertain 06

I'm through
with shrieking
like a monkey
at an eclipse
as the farways
are terrorizing
my pupil
the black
of a lava flow
our phosphor companions
glow illuminating
our hypocrites
and all that
we should envy
and feeding on my fear
they are erasing my
tomorrows
with flood and fire
and the religions
are ensuring
all their revelations
arrive
even if
at their own hands
cowards telling themselves
that they are compassionate
because they do
calisthenics under
a calcified corpse on Sunday
while shaping their voices
into thunder
to shame me
into a terrified animal

convincing me
that this cataclysm
is god.

and
the rationalists
are relying upon
the reasoning
of these superstitious;
their candles

while all around
is black and silence

I am certain
of no tomorrow
and
less certain
of yesterday

kojagra 06

who is awake?

I know better
in the morning
than to listen
to the many voices of night
with its edges
to tear upon
illuminated, sharpened
glistening with the rain
of the storm that
almost awakened me

but left me
a dish eyed
regressed simian
with its thunders
clinging to my blanket
and my flashlight,
my opposable thumb
inventions, that I pretend
can protect me
if I keep them within reach

a clumsy comfort
against
the rotation of the earth
is turning my stomach
bringing another night;
its delicate dangling
its treelike inability
to run

and the sky is swallowing me
even as skyscrapers
and church spires
attempt to hold the
blackness at bay
piercing it with their tips
if it dares approach
even thought its massive
body could crush them
like matchsticks
a horrifying mother.
but the only one i have
the only thing holding me,
from the streaks of light
that may find our direction

unsaid 06

the black of your pupil
never took
this

not until
another took it
and wore it
red
against the color
of their own eyes

and then
you apologized

for its spoken
in your
empirical dismissals,
the carefully controlled
pitch of your voice
and
slant of lip

and how your hands
never shook

in view.

but
despite those strategies,
still seen

in all this
unsaid

you tried
to take it back
by saying
less.

mirror 06

this mirror
does not let me
believe

in all it sees

in all it doesn't

unbroken
it causes more cuts
well-lit
it winces my eyes

and if I let
myself
self upon self upon self
linger there

it will mean
7 more years

monday mourning 06

pay no attention
to that ache
between your ribs
to that flutter
of a moths wings
upon a lightbulb
a breath
will shoo it away
and then bring
a swarm of others
and the hours
will trap it like
a lightning bug
in a jar
as we all squeeze through
the narrow middle
of the hour glass
all my imagined disasters
are making my footfalls
softer
and the monday morning air
is thick
upon my throat

seism 06

this single touch
along my ear,
a fault line slowly fissuring.
eruption under
depth of sea
that scattered schools
and shifted continents
into a map only
an inch askew
and still a new
world

and in its registering
upon the ocean
of each
displaced cell
I knew
the seismographs
wrote mad letters
in automatic writing
about what they sensed
from the other side
of the globe
while its ancient syllables
hit the nerve
of a elephants foot
and read itself
to a black eye
that searched
all of its
collective remembered
and found
no equivalent.

reshaped 06

the scent
was the first
to find her

that musk
of ozone earth
that rose
from the readily reshaped

and then her
throat knew it
and in closing
solitary inhale,
it told it to her eyes.

and there she was

her hands
small white spiders
consuming clay
recording a child's impulse
in its agile anatomy

and then erased
with another

these seconds
expanded and sent
from some
no more place
from some
no more time

from a her
she thought
overwritten
by this one

this precious 06

a rain refracted calliope
a glimmer distracted step
that hums with a
heavy head swaying
to the rhythm

of the shoves
of the afternoon's

downtown rudeness
that sways it
dropping peaches
on the pavement
with each swing
they fall
splattering into sunlight
from some
previously stored beautiful
that the thunder yells at
and lightning competes with

but only to punctuate
this precious

upon her umbrella lidded
eyes,her heart
outpaced her feet
with pulse
distorting her voice
with adrenaline
drugging her brain
with oversized chemicals
bubbling and barely
passing pillbugs migrating
through her skull,
tightening its skin
displacing any slack
left for surplus
cerebration vibration
dropping her neck
to the small of her back
to make a circle

of a now
that will never
reach a never.
her hips jutting to a
sonar's geography
broadcasted
to her internal organs
though bass
and basic
impulses pressing upon
fingertips searching the air
for edges of the force
pushing herself
to the back
of her own mind

disappearing 06

into the black
trusting the glowing
yellow lines

pausing only
in reverie of red lights
and gazing at the green
as a Gatsby
hoping

it's a sign;
but it's only a signal.

this road is lined
with too familiar fauna
each glisten,
each grass,
somehow their veins
still pulse
with an earlier passing
of me.

their roots
stretch for my wheels
but I stiffen my arm
and tighten my hand
on the wheel
chin up
gas pedal down.

I drown my sight
with each oncoming
radiance,
chasing all
the shadows
from my eyes,
from my retina,
from my nerve,
back to the back,
where they are buried
and belong
but

wait for traffic
to pass and with the radio
conspire
in resurrecting
my desire
and this wind washes
this wonder, will
wanting from
my brow
its last dangling
that holds only briefly
to the tangling
of my hair,

then to
the air,

and the night becomes
another disappearing

reaching 06

a thumb strumming
foot counting
the moments
in unknowing
subconscious sequence
and thighs
pulsing
to the missing of you

shivering all shown
from my eyes

I breathe in a smile
that closes my teeth,
dilating all other parts
of me

my tongue
searches my mouth
for company

while my arms
paralyze me
in a socially appropriate
manner
with a fist
to my throat,
another to my lap
and
my lips are still

reaching

hourly 06

how much time
are you worth?

paid by the dying,
a heartbeat
gradually slowing,
a past growing
and all the days
ahead
look just like
this one.

a serenade
moaning to a pulse
that the hours
and the ours
try to straighten
with regularity

for consistent quality
for uniform data flow
for reproducible originals

while this throb
globs, a gravy
and grabs
each inconsistency
in
each minute;

a drip
like a piano
considering alternate routes
to the same quiet
explosion.
of a song
that was written
in a 7 years old
sugar saturated,
over caffeinated
spinning dizzy
whistle
and murmur
of a made-up word

being made into another
with each slipped syllable

stumbling
to the next.

never thinking

how many hours
do I have left.

cut[h]is 06

I am not
strong enough
to exist

(not anymore)

in this shiver
I barely manage
not to
completely dissipate

(and escape)

instead I stroke
my forehead
as if there were
something to find

(some valve for pressure re-
lease)

but really
I'm just verifying
the physicality of my skin

it's there.

(still, still…)

a bandage
wrapped too tight
binding my bones
into a bundled
structure of human

(a sadistic swaddling)

it's there

( )

to hold me
in solitary

screaming at the raping
intrusion of
every nervous impulse
into the folds
of my brain

where I've managed
to hide

(from my hide)

hell is skin

science thinks it protection

(a vacuum sealed specimen)

but it's just
an open invitation
to destroyers

(a leverage for all levelers)

even my own fingernails
want to rip
through it

all its hungers
make me be

when I don't
want to.

heal thyself   06

"are you ok?"

I ask myself
with another's voice

to feed my veins
a self medicated
dose of concern,

a masturbatory mothering

that never comes
from another's lips.

I tend to myself

with a cup of coffee;
warming my hands
with it
my heat receptors
react and spread
the rumor
up my arms
causing them to bend
and my body to curl
forward
in intent listening,

even as my
palms and fingers
shriek
that they are burning.

I keep them there.

sacrificing
the prints of my fingertips
to relieve this frostbite;

this cold that numbs
all things
but knowing.

"no I'm not

but I WILL be..."

continuing 06

my body has learned,
despite me,
that certain sensations
are to be
ignored.

for closure and continuity;
for continuing.

the rough clothing
against my skin;
its uncomfortable
creases and folds
when I'm bloated.
the smell of my skin.
the smell of your skin.
the smell of exhaust.
the hum of machines
working themselves
to life.
the imperfect thump
of the road.
the cricks and creeks
of old vinyl 33s.
the heater rumbling
in my sleep.
the taste of old coffee.
the taste of my teeth.

the way news lies.
the way god is evil.

the way you hate me.

pendulum 06

and I am
counting
my nevers
with a sway
that tries
to remind
my
floating mind
of oceans,
of wombs.

each tick

of my metronome
torso
notes
all the possibles
that I doubted;

forcing
blood through
this cold,
sating thirsty nerves,

teasing until
another dry season
another ice age

forces my survival
to seek a
subterranean
well.

the wild 06

behind these eyes,
the wild.

the hide
that knows to hide
and has warmed
itself
in wetter winters
than your alones.

the nostrils
that smell the blood
on you
before
your lips
are close enough
to lie to me

the dark, the still
of a stare
that does not care

but when the hunters
come

knows
some form of worse
will worsen
beyond its ability
to react

so it never retracts

the dull glare
of sight tracing
the features of your face,
the figment,

but can hear
the creeping
at slow slaughtering paces
through the leaves,

the want
you think
can wean me

from the wild.

smell the ocean 06

as soon as
I speak the truth
I know
the world has lied
to me

but something else
has caught my breath
and delivered
upon it
an expanse
to this
enclosed.

I can smell the ocean.

over the
tarred and tainted,
the gasolines
and summer sheens
of walls of windows,
over the
cheap cologne
of the over-pheromonal
and sweat
of all that chases me
to pick my pocket
and steal my senses;

I can still smell the ocean.

the salt
that means open air,
the shoreward wind
that carries
a wide whisper
whose wake
is here
to wake me.
the inner infinite
of its shells
have spiraled
into me.

over the
shapes cemented to sky,
over trees,
over there,
my eyes cannot see passed.
a surf that surfaced
and silenced in the air,
no longer in the
nautilus of my ear;
only its chill
but not its sand
upon my skin,
only its simulated
tips my tongue.

but I can still smell the ocean.

Made in the USA
Charleston, SC
04 June 2011